NATIONAL GEOGRAPHIC

Ladders

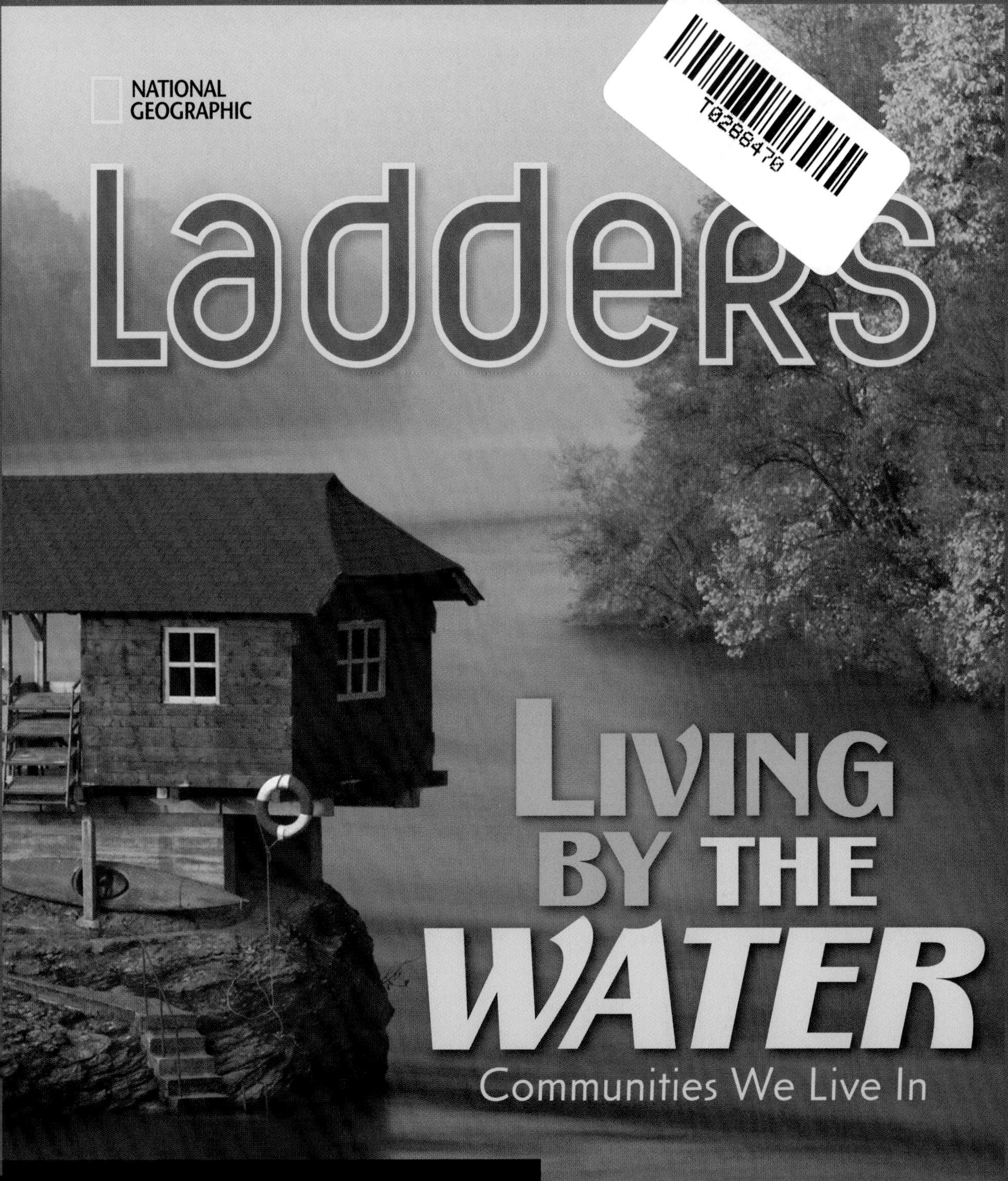

Living by the Water

Communities We Live In

2 **Rescue a River** *Narrative*
by Becky Manfredini

10 **Brace for Impact** *Social Studies Article*
by Mattie Jaffe

16 **A City by the Water** *Opinion Piece*
by Mattie Jaffe and Ann Wildman

24 **Discuss**

GENRE Narrative **Read to find out** about the Colorado River.

RESCUE A RIVER

by Becky Manfredini

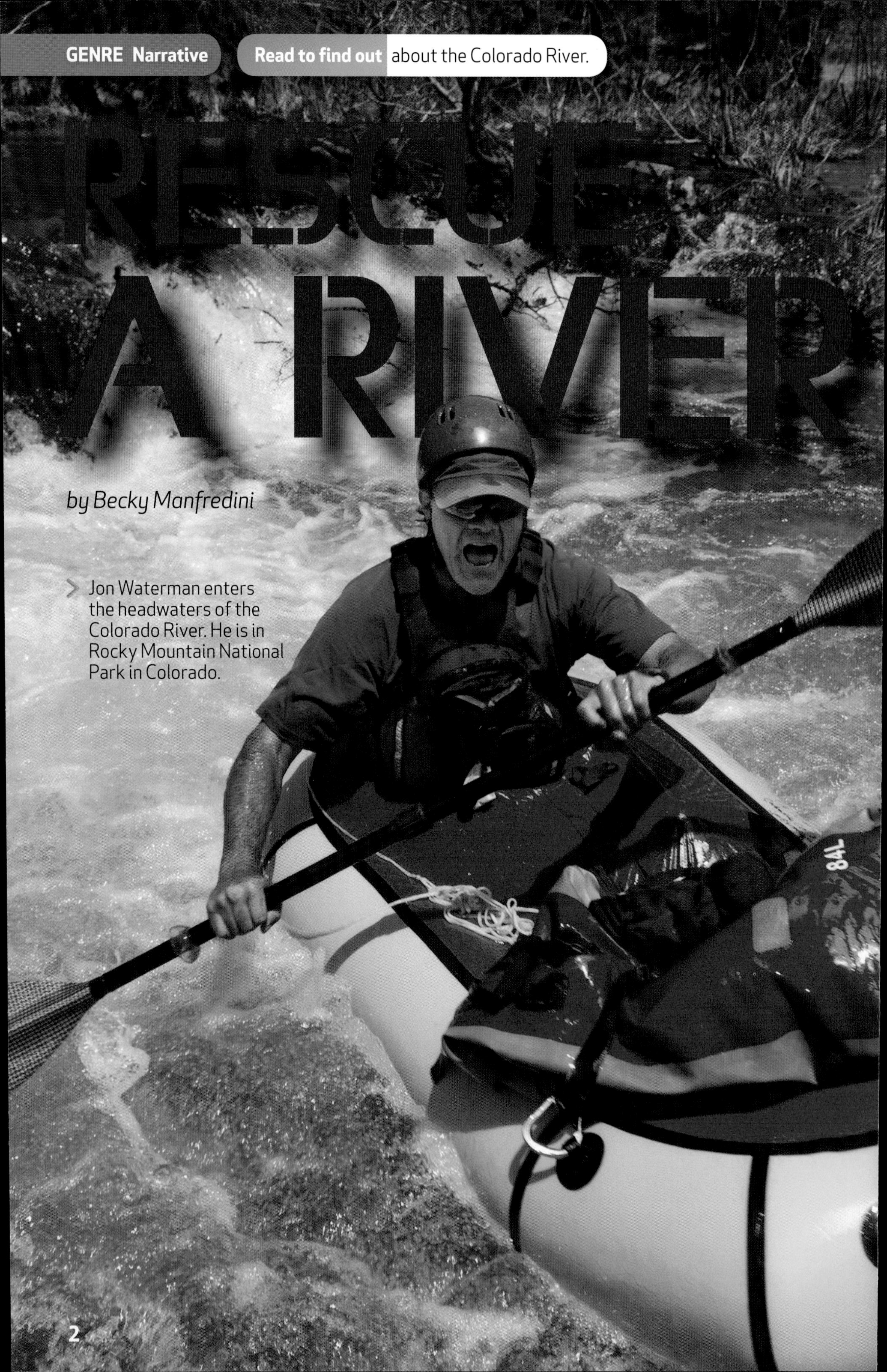

Jon Waterman enters the headwaters of the Colorado River. He is in Rocky Mountain National Park in Colorado.

Jon Waterman and Pete McBride are writers and photographers. One day in 2008, they packed their rafts for a long journey down the Colorado River. The men slid their rafts into the river in the mountains of Colorado. They were at the **headwaters**, or the beginning, of the river. Jon and Pete knew farms and communities were using a lot of water from the river. They wanted to see firsthand how this was affecting the river and those who depend on its water.

Jon would spend 150 days paddling 1,450 miles. Pete would join Jon for parts of the trip. Together they would explore the white-water rapids and calm waters. But Pete wanted to see the river from above, too. So he took pictures of it from a plane.

Jon and Pete saw many different types of land on their trip. They saw the bright city of Las Vegas. They saw the high cliffs of the Grand Canyon and the flat deserts of Mexico. But the land wasn't the only thing that changed along the Colorado River. The river itself changed.

Jon Waterman travels around the world. He writes about the ways people can protect our planet.

Pete McBride uses a special camera when he takes photographs from a raft. His cameras are sealed so that water cannot leak inside them.

THE MIGHTY COLORADO RIVER

For six million years, the Colorado River flowed swiftly through the western United States and Mexico. Plants and fish filled its waters. But as the population grew in the Southwest, more people began using the river's water. Today, more than 30 million people depend on the Colorado River. They use it for drinking, showering, and other reasons. However, farms use most of the river's water, which is pumped from the river to grow crops on farms as far away as California.

Jon checks out smaller rivers that flow into the Colorado River. This is the Rio Hardy. The word *rio* means river in Spanish.

On their trip in 2008, Jon and Pete saw that the river's water level was dropping. In fact, the Colorado River has dropped about 130 feet since 2000. That means less water is flowing than before. Today, scientists worry that droughts and hot weather will cause even less water to flow through this river. Droughts are times of little or no rainfall. Many people depend on the Colorado River's water. Will there be enough water in the river if droughts continue?

THE COLORADO RIVER

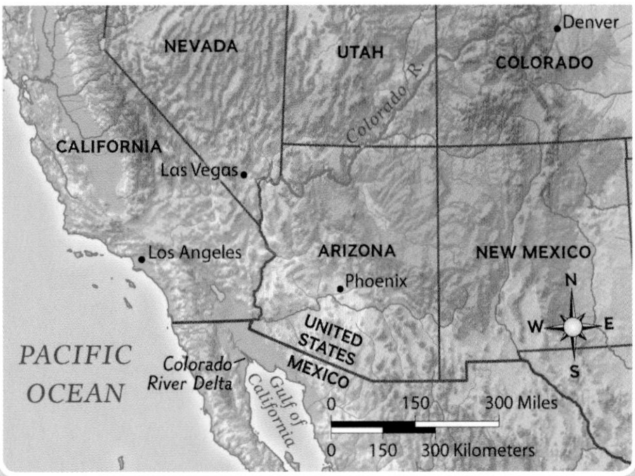

A DISAPPEARING RIVER

Jon and Pete paddled way down the Colorado River. Inside the country of Mexico, the once-clear water turned into mud. The mud was so thick that their rafts got stuck. The men had to push their rafts out with their paddles.

The men wondered if the mud would reach all the way to the river's **delta**. A delta is land built up by loose dirt that the river has carried to the sea. Until 1998, the Colorado River flowed all the way to the Gulf of California. It flowed through a grassy delta before pouring into the gulf. This delta was filled with colorful birds and other wildlife. Today, it is less than 10 percent of its original size. That is

because the Colorado River is polluted and no longer flows to the Gulf of California. Mud has replaced the grass and flowing water. The animals that used to live there have gone elsewhere.

Jon and Pete had to stop rafting before they reached the gulf. The river dried up and disappeared. They carried their rafts on their backs. As the men looked around, they couldn't help but worry. More than 300,000 birds stop along the river delta each year. They rest here on their way to warmer places. But if the river delta is not cleaned up, the birds won't have a healthy place to rest in the future.

In Mexico, the once-clear water of the Colorado River is now muddy and filled with trash.

WHAT COMMUNITIES CAN DO

One reason Jon and Pete made this trip was to show how important the Colorado River is to animals. The men want to **conserve**, or protect, the river. People can conserve by using less water to grow crops and water lawns and keeping the river clean. Then plants and animals won't lose their homes. Jon and Pete are writing books and making movies. They are asking people to save the Colorado River.

The men's trip down the Colorado River also teaches us how important rivers are to people. Rivers carry **fresh water** to farms, towns, and cities. Fresh water contains little salt. It is good for growing food, drinking, and washing. We need to make sure there will always be plenty of fresh water.

Jon carries his belongings on his back. He is walking across a dry stretch where the Colorado River used to flow to get to a place where the river is still flowing.

CONSERVE OUR PLANET'S FRESH WATER

Conserve water at home. Limit the use of tap water for showers and brushing your teeth. Use plants in your lawn that don't need a lot of water. And only water your lawn early or late in the day.

Pick up litter around rivers and lakes. Polluted water harms animals. Polluted water can't be used by communities.

Turn off lights when they're not in use. Power plants use water to create electricity. If you use less electricity, power plants can make less electricity and use less water.

Eat less meat. Farms use water to grow crops that feed animals being raised as food. Animals also need to drink water. If you eat less meat, fewer animals will be raised as food. Less water will be necessary to raise them.

Check In Explain what is happening to the water in the Colorado River. Why does the river need to be saved?

GENRE **Social Studies Article**

Read to find out how different members of a river community worked together in an emergency.

Brace for

IT WAS THE AFTERNOON OF JANUARY 15, 2009.

The 155 passengers and crew members aboard U.S. Airways Flight 1549 fastened their seat belts. At 3:25 p.m., the plane took off from New York's LaGuardia Airport. It was headed to Charlotte, North Carolina.

Less than two minutes after the plane left the ground, passenger Eric Stevenson looked out the window next to his seat on the plane. He noticed a flock of geese flying next to the airplane. Seconds later he heard some loud thuds and smelled something burning.

At the plane's controls were Captain Chesley "Sully" Sullenberger and copilot Jeff Skiles. They knew that the plane had flown through a flock of Canada geese. Some of the birds had been sucked into the engines, and the plane had lost power.

Passengers make their way onto the plane's wings. They wait to be rescued from the middle of New York's Hudson River.

IMPACT

by Mattie Jaffe

Skiles tried to restart the engines, but nothing worked. There was no time to return to the airport. Captain Sullenberger would have to make an emergency landing. But where? Then he saw a wide, open space below them. It was the Hudson River. Landing there would be dangerous. But it was their only choice.

Captain Sullenberger made a calm announcement on the loudspeaker. He said, "Brace for impact." Passengers prepared themselves. They leaned forward and placed their feet flat on the floor.

Captain Sullenberger fell in love with flying and airplanes when he was a boy. Later, he became a pilot in the United States Air Force. As a pilot, Sully always put safety first. He also taught people how to fly planes safely. After the event on the Hudson River, Sully began working with the Young Eagles, a group that teaches children about airplanes.

A MIRACLE ON THE HUDSON

Less than six minutes after takeoff, the huge plane dropped onto the Hudson River in New York City.

Sully was a very experienced pilot. He knew to ease the plane slowly onto the water. He didn't want the plane to flip when it hit the water. He also didn't want to land too slowly and crash the plane nose-first. Sully landed the plane perfectly. The quick thinking of Sully and his crew saved everyone on board the plane.

Emergency workers put on scuba gear so they can dive into the freezing water.

Firefighters throw a rope to passengers. The rope is used to secure the raft.

Landing the plane on the water also protected the people of New York City. This big city is packed tight with buildings and people. Suppose the plane had gone down on land. Many more people's lives could have been in danger.

As soon as the plane hit the Hudson, the **waterway** sprang to life. Coast Guard workers spotted passengers waiting on the plane's wings. Rescue boats sped to help the passengers. **Ferryboats**, which normally carry people back and forth across the wide river, raced toward the plane, too. The passengers could see that New Yorkers would rescue them quickly. They were wet and cold, but they were alive!

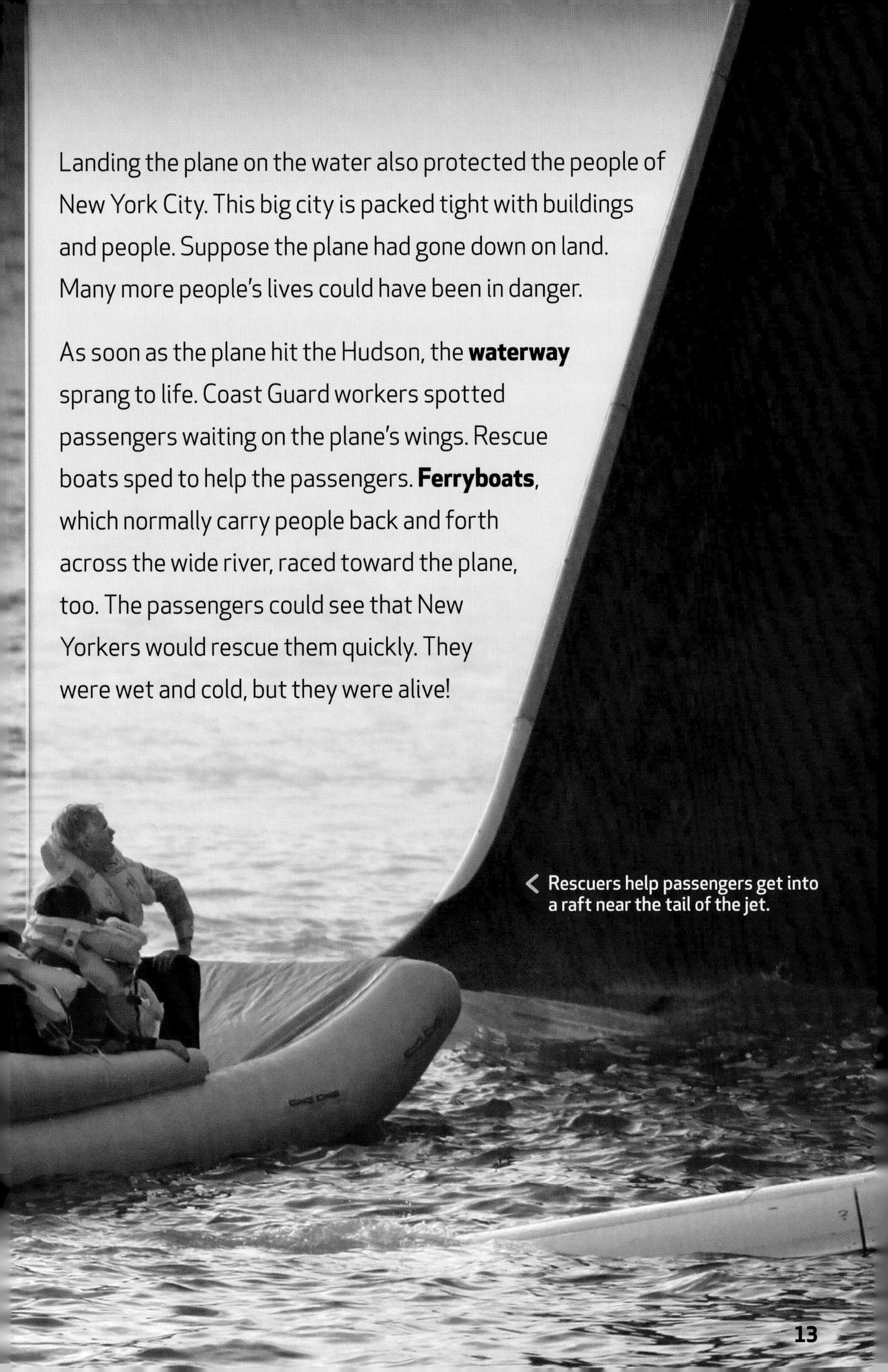

Rescuers help passengers get into a raft near the tail of the jet.

COMING TOGETHER

The plane's passengers were taken aboard the rescue boats. Workers gave them warm clothing. The boats brought the plane's passengers to shore.

Then the people on land stepped up to help out. Restaurants welcomed hungry passengers. Nurses and doctors at local hospitals cared for passengers who had been hurt.

Many different types of boats help in the rescue.

New Yorkers came together and showed the passengers of Flight 1549 how much they cared.

People called Captain Sullenberger a hero. However, Sully praised his crew. "I was very happy that everyone involved did their jobs extraordinarily well."

Check In What caused the plane to crash?

GENRE Opinion Piece

Read to find out about the pros and cons of living in New Orleans.

A City by

by Mattie Jaffe and Ann Wildman

Just Call Me "NOLA." Listen and you'll catch the lively sound of a trumpet playing a tune. Breathe in and smell the fresh seafood gumbo. Watch a 100-year-old riverboat splash by on the Mississippi River. You're in New Orleans, Louisiana, or "NOLA," as people call this city on the water.

New Orleans is almost surrounded by water. The city lies along the Mississippi River. Several lakes and the Gulf of Mexico are also nearby. New Orleans has been an important **port** since the 1700s. A port is a place on the water where ships load and unload goods. Around 6,000 ships travel along the Mississippi each year. They bring boxes of goods

the Water

A look at New Orleans from across the Mississippi River

in and out of New Orleans. This shipping gives many people jobs to do.

When they aren't working, the people of New Orleans have fun along the water. But summers in New Orleans can be very hot and steamy. Hurricanes, big storms with strong winds, sometimes threaten the city during the fall. New Orleans can be a stormy place to live!

The French Quarter is a very old neighborhood in New Orleans. It is known for its historic buildings.

A Stormy City

In August 2005, weather forecasters tracked a growing hurricane in the Gulf of Mexico. Would it hit New Orleans? On August 29, it did. The strength of the hurricane named Katrina caught many people by surprise. Within hours, cars looked like submarines under rising floodwaters. Trees were flattened. Houses were destroyed. Many people had no electricity.

What caused all of this damage? Strong winds up to 170 miles-per-hour caused Gulf waters to rise. Eventually, the water spilled over the **levee** walls. Levees were built around New Orleans to protect it from flooding. Everyone knew that a bad flood could hit low-lying New Orleans. But they thought the levees would help. Unfortunately, Katrina was just too powerful.

Hurricane Katrina caused 80 percent of New Orleans to flood.

Once the storm passed, help was on the way. The American Red Cross, a group that helps people in need, provided meals and safe places to stay. Volunteer workers gave families clothing and groceries. Other helpers built safe homes for people whose homes were destroyed by Hurricane Katrina.

It took several years, but New Orleans became a thriving city again. Visitors soon returned to enjoy the things that make New Orleans special. The levees were also strengthened. People hope the levees will keep New Orleans safe next time a storm hits.

Hurricane Katrina was the largest hurricane to hit the United States.

A volunteer saws lumber. He is helping rebuild a home near New Orleans.

Down on the Bayou

When it isn't storming, people in New Orleans spend time outside. Sometimes they visit the **bayou** (BY-oo). Bayous are marshy, slow-moving streams. There are many bayous near New Orleans.

Would you like to see the animals and plants of the bayou? Sign up for a swamp tour! You can hop aboard a boat for a calm and quiet ride. Or you can take a special boat called an airboat. Airboats are small boats with a large fan on the back. Air blasts through the fan to blow the boat across the water.

^ The bayous near New Orleans are home to many alligators.

v In the fall, some trees in the bayou turn orange.

Keep your eyes open. You'll notice soft strands of moss that seem to drip from the tree branches. These mossy trees have strong roots that grow together into a wall below the water. The root walls help keep floodwaters out of cities such as New Orleans.

In the bayou, the bugs swarm around you like a thick cloud. There are plenty of animals to see, too. Alligators live in the bayous. So do egrets. These are large, beautiful wading birds. And don't miss the nutria. They look a little like beavers with long, rat-like tails. It's amazing that this wild setting is so close to a big city like New Orleans.

Let Loose

New Orleans is known for one of the liveliest parties in the country. It is called Mardi Gras (MAHR-dee GRAH). This huge party happens before a long holiday of fasting, or not eating certain foods. Mardi Gras is a chance for large crowds to eat and have fun.

Some of the best parts of Mardi Gras are the parades. People wear fancy costumes and glittery masks. They hop on the floats and toss gifts such as plastic necklaces and coins to the crowd. These gifts are called "throws." Kids dress up in funny costumes hoping to get more throws. Throws are good luck.

Anyone can join special Mardi Gras parades called "second line parades." They feature musicians playing **jazz**.

Jazz is a special type of music. It has a strong beat and uses instruments such as horns, drums, and pianos. In a second line parade, the sounds of the horns and drums catch people's attention. Parade watchers can join in the fun by dancing behind the musicians.

New Orleans is a city near the water. It can have storms and flooding. However, jazz, good food, parades, and adventures in the bayous make living in New Orleans exciting.

People spend all year building floats. Floats are made of wood and plaster.

Street bands lead dancers in a second line parade.

Check In Name one reason someone might want to live in New Orleans. Name one reason someone might not want to live there.

Discuss

1. What connects the three selections that you read in this book?

2. How do the communities along the Colorado River use the river's water? What are some ways communities such as yours can conserve water from rivers and lakes?

3. How did the water community of New York City work together to rescue the passengers of Flight 1549?

4. How does the location of New Orleans affect the people who live there?

5. What do you still wonder about living by the water?

Glossary

bayou (noun) a slow-moving stream in the southeastern United States

conserve (verb) to not be wasteful or harmful

delta (noun) a deposit of earth and sand that collects at the mouths of some rivers

ferryboat (noun) a water vehicle that carries people and goods across a river or a lake

fresh water (noun) water that is not salty

headwaters (noun) the sources of a river

jazz (noun) a type of music that has a strong beat, originating in the southern United States

levee (noun) walls built on either side of a river to prevent flooding

port (noun) a place on the water where ships load and unload goods

waterway (noun) a river, canal or other channel of water that ships can travel through

NATIONAL GEOGRAPHIC

SOCIAL STUDIES

Ladders

Communities We Live In Series

- Living in the Desert
- Living in the Mountains
- Living on the Plains
- Living by the Water
- Living on the Coast

Acknowledgments
Andrew J. Milson
Social Studies Consultant

Grateful acknowledgment is given to the authors, artists, photographers, museums, publishers, and agents for permission to reprint copyrighted material. Every effort has been made to secure the appropriate permission. If any omissions have been made or if corrections are required, please contact the Publisher.

Credits
Wrap Cover, Title Page (bg) ©Irene Becker/National Geographic Stock. **Front Cove**r (bl) ©Peter McBride/National Geographic Stock. (bc) ©Steven Day/AP Images. (br) ©Henryk Sadura/Getty Images. **Back Cover** (tl) ©Kyle Krause/Photolibrary/Getty Images. **2-8** ©Peter McBride/ National Geographic Stock. **9** (c) ©Picture Partners/age fotostock. **10** (bg) ©Steven Day/AP Images. **11** (tr) ©Andrew Theodorakis/NY Daily News Archive via Getty Images. **12-15** ©Eric Thayer/Reuters. **16** (bg) ©Henryk Sadura/Getty Images. **17** (br) ©José Fuste Raga/age fotostock. **18** (bg) ©Tyrone Turner/National Geographic Stock. **19** (tr) ©Stocktrek Images/Getty Images. (br) ©Cheryl Gerber/AP Images for Rebuilding Together. **20** (bg) ©Frank Krahmer/Corbis. (cl) ©Kyle Krause/ Photolibrary/Getty Images. **22** (bg) ©Joe Vogan/Alamy. **23** (tr) ©Matthew D White/Peter Arnold/Getty Images. **24** (bg) ©Henryk Sadura/Getty Images. (tl) ©Steven Day/AP Images. (tr) ©Peter McBride/National Geographic Stock. All maps provided by Mapping Specialists.

Visit National Geographic Learning online at www.NGL.cengage.com
Visit our corporate website at www.cengage.com

Printed in the USA.

RR Donnelley, Menasha, WI

ISBN: 978-1-2853-4800-1

14 15 16 17 18 19 20 21 22

10 9 8 7 6 5 4 3 2 1

111

NATIONAL GEOGRAPHIC

Ladders

710L

NGL.Cengage.com 888-915-3276

ISBN 978-1-2853-4800-1

90000

9 781285 348001

NATIONAL GEOGRAPHIC LEARNING | CENGAGE Learning